WHISPERS IN THE VELVET BLUE

CHRISTIE LEIGH BABIRAD

Second Edition.

ISBN: 978-1-963705-86-7

Cover images: Adobestock

Interior images: © Christie Leigh Babirad

Published in the United States of America by Harbor Lane Books, LLC.

www.harborlanebooks.com

Whispers in the Velvet Blue is dedicated to my mom, Cheryl Suzanne, for inspiring me to continually live soulfully and always supporting my heart's journey, no matter where it takes me.

HONEY

Your presence
in my everyday
like honey,
pressing into every space of my heart.

There is no pattern.
There is no method to your love.
You've simply come in
and sweetly inhabited this house
ever so completely.

Daydreams

Where do the daydreams go if you remember them all?

Do they go into stories and art that have yet to be shown, or into wishes that have been destined to still come true?

I still see the Ferris wheel on the beach that the hurricane later washed away.

I was thirteen, and I had imagined a boy I never did meet, taking me there.

We would weave through the carnival excitement and then sit in the sands by the ocean as an orange sun set in the sky.

This was to be my first kiss,
my first love.

We would come back at sunrise to have breakfast
together on the beach since we were both coming from
just down the street.

I would carry two bottled waters and two bagels in one
of those brown paper bags for him and for me.

It would be my treat because I had imagined him
becoming my meant-to-be.

IN THE STILL

We never touched,
so why can't I get you off my mind,
still?
I do know the answer.
It's because I imagined your touch in every detail so
many times...

Rough
Softening for me
Cautious
Assured when you knew that's what I needed you
to be
Safe
Home
Complete.

In the still you cross my mind all the time.
My goodness, you could dance too!
This wasn't because you had danced before, but
because you wanted to.
You wanted to move with me.
Coming in so close with your hands on my hips,
you were this consuming wall of love that became such
a big part of me.

I wrapped my arms loosely around you because I never
felt you leaving.
Your kiss was never small.
It was like riding a giant wave while the summer sun
painted your skin from head to toe for the first time
after many seasons having passed.

My head spins thinking about all that I felt with you.
In the still, I hurt so deeply with these thoughts.
I can't replace this with any other man.
There was something so strong about you,
and this ache that I feel will always belong to you.

I have to let you go,
I know.

I don't want to think of you any longer, but please

know how much you deserve to be loved, the way I
wanted to love you, and all that is more.
In the still, I wish today for every one of your dreams
to come true,
and for you to always know how much I cared for you.

There will never be any doubt that your love for me
was as real as
anything could be.

SOMETHING MORE

Walking,
feeling so completely tethered—
Like I have to teach myself to breathe once again,
since you took my hand,
when we were standing on that concert hall floor
with all the different rays of light shining down,
and all the other stories crowded around.
We only met a few hours ago,
but my fingers slid so naturally between yours.
My hand was in your hand,
and your kiss I couldn't resist.
Now, I can't forget.
Songs I have heard so many times before,
now I can't hear any of them without thinking of you.
Every tender touch and every glance,

I wish I could come through to you,
because this couldn't have been meant for just one
night.
When you put your hand on my back,
you touched me with the fragility I felt inside.
Everything that has happened before,
somehow it seemed you already understood.
The way you looked into me,
out of the corner of my eye I couldn't deny the spark.
I knew I was going to need you.
And others can think that it's way too soon to feel the
way I do.
I honestly think it's crazy too.
You left with my name,
and I left with something more it seems.
I'm fighting to forget the memories,
but wishing all the same.
My dream,
that one day soon you'll come back to me.

Moved

I fell in love today.
With the flap of a page,
my life was no longer the same.

My lips parted.
I breathed in,
then out
a sigh.

Your words,
a dancing worm into my heart,
and I said,
"Yes."

DECEMBER

Icicle lights,
creamy delights,
mean so much more with you
by my side.

I Think of You

You're the one I think of.
When nothing seems to be going right,
you're the one who could make everything better.
You're a sharp blue ray through the darkness,
loving me like I've never been loved before.
I'm going to love you,
beyond my last breath,
beyond earthly constraints.
Pink Roses...
Blue Jeans...
Kisses Beneath the Orange...
Whenever I feel that I can't go on,
you remind me of a love that won't simply fade away.
You have me hearing the electric guitar...
piano keys...

the wailing of a saxophone playing to the night...

high notes all the way through...

the drum tapped to just the right rhythm.

And I see the waters of Capri with you.

I see the open road...

country driving...

a velvet green...

and the city lights of Paris while feeling the sweetest

rain falling on us.

Someday I know that you will come my way.

Until that most wonderful day,

I will continue to think of you.

Foreign Love

A young girl,
I didn't know too much about anything,
but oh, how you made my heart sing!

I knew the memory of you would be more lasting than
any ring.

The salt air was swept into me like a wave covering
over me.

The scent of your sharp cologne on that white
undershirt as I hid behind you
is a feeling
I will never forget.

Like playing dress-up in layers of pearls,
I knew deep in my soul somehow,
I fit the role.

We were a forbidden love,
foreign to my heart and the different sands we each
stood on,
but in that time and faraway place,
we were positively one.

HOPE

As I weave through the ups and downs of this life of
mine,
all the places I've been,
and the place where I've always stayed,
I come back to this same heart.
And this song makes me feel,
there's a nightlight within
glowing through this chaotic trail of mine.
Leading me to the next path,
I believe,
this is where I'm going to dance all day and night.
I'll be led into all the new adventures ahead
shining a little brighter the further I go.

DEAR MUSE

I know you think you're being cute,
waking me up in the middle of the night,
making me turn on that bright light.
I admit that most times I really do like you too.
In the daylight I often try and desperately chase you.
But now I'm trying to sleep.
You picked quite the funny time to go deep.
My goodness, I feel as if you're laughing at me!
You know that I can't deny the vision you always see.
My beauty rest is what I need,
but here I go once again off to follow your lead.

Laramie

You waved to us on that dirt road as we drove away.
A figment of my imagination?
I don't know.
But the memory is vivid and holds tightly of you, a boy
I didn't even know.
And I wonder to this day whether this was goodbye,
or an assurance that I'd see you again one day.
It's one of those fairy-winged moments in life,
going beyond the ordinary into the existentially sweet.
I was tied to your land and sky,
even though I couldn't place why.
We only spent a few days,
but I remember the tears that filled my eyes in that
backseat as we pulled away that sunny day.

I could only look at you once before the pain of already
longing took over.

The heartache remains when I think of Laramie under
these big city lights,

making me still wonder if this was goodbye,

or if I will one day once again find my way back to you.

SUPERSTAR

There's a well-known superstar who reminds me of you. The similarities are even in the way he moves. The songs he sings are your groove, but the fact remains that he could never be you.

I often think about what could have been. I had a vision for your future before I figured out my own. I saw you as a star who would never have me stray too far. We would complement each other, never letting ourselves forget who we are.

I hope that you are happy wherever you are, and that you know that for you I will never be too far. I still miss you. I do. I at times purposely watch him on the screen to remember you, but the truth will always remain, in my heart he could never be as great as you.

THE BUBBLE

Time and time again you have told me that the bubble
is where it's at,
and as storytellers we must find this for our life to have
the dexterity of a cat.
It's a comfort spot that takes over all of you,
where love meets true,
and nothing and no one else can come in to make you
blue.
But I go back to his pool,
diving for iridescent pink, blue, and green jewels.
I felt this magic you speak of, but when he departed, I
was left feeling like one of the fools.
For the bubble is sweet and fulfilling for a while,
but like a protective glass case your mamma says she'd
like to put you in sometimes,

this space leaves no room to grow in life's naturally dynamic and expansive flow.

ON REPEAT

He has a voice that makes me think of you,
bringing those good memories back,
of the way you would take my hand to pull me
into you.
In my heart,
I may be making you cooler than you were.
But to me you came in with a giant bright red umbrella
in the middle of a storm.
You didn't overthink what I may or may not need,
with a sexy assuredness and getting-to-know-you
questions you would seek.
So now I listen to his songs to hold onto what I loved
about you.
For when the meant-to-be-forever guy comes my way,

I'll have you to thank for pulling out a side of me I so desperately needed to free.

Taking Flight

She's taking flight,
with dreams and songs on her mind,
to rescue her heart.

Perfect Timing

Early morning

Dark sky

Driving

I hear our stream rushing

Invigorated by thoughts of you

But there's plenty of time

I see our sunset

Stirring faith in my heart of God's promise

This vision can't be denied

And I know

It's so early in my story

But there's a strong belief in us now

And I'd wait forever

'Cause we are sure to be extraordinary

With our perfect timing

OUR SCENE

Fade In:

Opening take of you and me.

We're one,

not two.

Sapphire starred sky,

into your chest I sigh.

This we don't even have to try.

Barely stepping in this dance,

I'll never regret this chance.

Salt swirling in November air,

you hold me close, stirring a flurry of emotions.

But every dotted star is out tonight,

making me feel

everything happening is absolutely right.

ENCHANTED

Enigmatic to outwardly obtain this feeling.
Next to impossible to define outside the realm of
emotion.
Coloring the spirit in iridescent fairy-like sparkle.

Holding the deepest love firmly ahead of any and all
darkness.

Amazing it is to carry this view in your heart every day.

Never could it be an act of foolishness.

Taking you into abundance if you believe.

Emptying less than deep care from your soul.

Dynamically changing all that it touches as it opens the
great power of possibility

until you fully become what it means to be—

ENCHANTED.

SPIRIT

There's so much she wants.
There's so much she needs.
It's just beyond reason,
just past practical.
She dwells in a rich land of possibility
the "grown" often turn their noses up to at first spark.
She's the one who can't let go of the hands on her
heart,
the ones lasting,
and the ones meant to part.
There is an all too powerful wave of energetic light
rushing through her,
incessantly urging that she keep journeying for the
mystical and the magical,
for truth.

It's the 'why' she feels every touch.
Not dissimilar to the wild Mustang who bucks at that which is unsettling,
her spirit will always break free from the all too ridden ground.

Sapphire Stars

Sapphire stars are in her eyes.
She thinks this must be far greater than love.
Love has become too casual a word these days,
and difficult it is to draw the line
between infatuation and true.
In sapphire stars she sees
a visualization of the power she feels
when she is with you.
She is illuminated.
There is an energy to the breeze that surrounds
this union of souls.
And like fireworks in the night sky,
there are so many places to look
when your heart is wide open.
She has to put her camera down,

pause,

to feel the expansion.

With his hands and arms holding her so close,

chest to chest,

heartbeat to heartbeat,

it's a passion that's forever—if not forgotten.

She knows she can't hold on too tightly,

but that she can't let go.

Bright in color,

her body has become,

with sapphire stars in her eyes

eternally for you.

THIS TIME OF YEAR

Lying in a field of green velvet.
Staring at a great big sky,
Covered in blankets of orange and pink.
Captivated by the surrounding beauty,
The colors increasingly vivid with each hour.
There's magic in the air tonight,
I can feel it in my bones.
Excitement builds for what's ahead.
On the lingering chill wafts the scent of firewood.
Piano keys play sweet melodies in the surrounding
stillness of my heart.
Violet satin dresses,
White roses,
This season is made for dreamers like me.

The rest of the year's insecurities plague me no more.
Mistakes made, lessons learned,
I find a new strength and hope in today.

Rendezvous Road

The road tugged at me again,
us both knowing
it is only this that can clear the congestion in our
minds.
We set out at two in the morning
with the black night and white light.
Gliding into the gentle break of day,
warm blues, oranges, and pinks greeted us.
The sky then morphed into a day of solid color.
We recorded green mile markers in our minds,
and took in the land that was everywhere we looked.
Hearts began to beat wildly again,
and I reached into my bag for my notebook and pen,
over and over again.
I pulled out my camera too

to capture
openness,
expansiveness,
the sky deepening into darker shades
'til the stars shined
in all these new places.

Konza Prairie

Sifting through pictures
of land I was a part of.
I've seen the bright blue waters of Hawaii.
I've seen the breathtaking cathedrals of Italy and Spain.
But none of these places hold the thick aroma of soil
on the summer winds across the Konza Prairie Lands.
No other place has me aching to sink into love

with the sight of a golden-winged butterfly pausing on
a blade of grass,
making sure I internalize this moment.
No other place has me mentally digging those roots.
All that matters,
singing to me
like the electric guitar solo in a country love song.
There's freedom in finding a home that viscerally
belongs to you.
This is a place in my heart that I know will never let go.

LOST IN THE SKY

I'm lost in the sky
with its winter steel blues.
The seagulls are flying low.
A storm is coming.
I can feel it in my bones,
and I'm excited!
I have a wish that passion will intensify
with the collective energy that's said to exist.
I want to hear the steady heartbeats all around me
come alive!
Maybe then we can be friends,
if only for a little while.
It's then that maybe I won't feel so out of place.
I rush to my destination,

high on desire.
Words swirl in my lungs.
I want to capture the exact color before it fades away.
The sky always beautiful,
but never the same twice.

FIRE

She can only take so much.
Seeing a whole lot more now,
transfixed in a constant state of motion,
home isn't one place or even two.
Trying to tie her down will only give strength for
breaking free.
Practical might as well be stagnant.

Incomparable empathy,
don't mistake love for an advantage.
She's aware of the dark.
Hurt many times,
it may be forgiven,
but you can bet it's not forgotten.

Continually melting into a melody,
she recognizes the silence.

Unpredictable at times,
she's looking to have only what's real,
nothing superficial will remain.

A kiss in the pouring rain would be perfect,
or maybe a long run on the beach as the season's first
snow falls.
Feeling alive is all that matters to her.

A playlist planned,
driving through the night,
always falling deeper than expected,
rising to an unsteady beat.
She's simply defined:
FIRE!

A GIFT

Your fingers intertwined with mine,
palm against palm,
arms touching,
I try to feel again,
and I long for us to be together,
not apart.
Picturing every detail,
I hear your words and the background music,
and capture every moment once more
as the rain falls in the sunshine,
the only kind of light I like.
I know you would already understand why
I detach myself from this world.
Heavenly emotions filling me
like a clear blue stream,

and I don't want to leave this place.
Until I see you again,
I'll remember the touch of your hand on my back
through my dark green coat,
and once more I'll feel your lips on mine.
To have this magic right now,
I would give you all of me,
to believe in beautiful,
the way you made me feel.
You're a gift I long to open forever,
not once,
not just a memory.

My Love

You are with me tonight
as the hands on the clock turn back,
my life continually filled
with memories of you.

Our story has no past,
and there is nothing seen ahead.

In this moment with you,
when I left, I didn't realize how much I would
miss you.

I miss you.

You are Valentine Red,

a kiss that never touched my lips
but was felt more than any that ever had.

And when I close my eyes,
you are right here still,
your cologne and the crisp ocean air.

And I feel you holding me,
like all those years ago.
I belong to you.
You belong to me.
I still feel this way.

You need to know,
your goodbye never left me.
The way you ran after me not expecting a thing to
change;
your love was so true,
like poetry.
My Love,
tonight, it's just another night I wish for you.

A Lasting
Connection

I ache when you cross my mind,
and the daydreams escape me too soon.
I know it's wrong to feel the way I do.
I should have let you go by now.
It's no good to feel this empty inside.

Closing my eyes tight,
I try to force myself into a deep sleep,
to dream a little longer.

It's no use.

I'm running on nothing but a memory.

I still feel,

your touch on the small of my back,
your kiss wanting more,
the music and lights from that night,
the heat of needing
this burning connection of two souls into one.

I still remember,
a goodbye that signaled
this is not an end.

MY ESCAPE

Can you be the one to give me something to believe in
again?
Will you be someone I can count on when I can't see a
thing?
I told you about my need to leave.
Could you be the one to start the car?
We could run away to the sea.
We could live among those who still dream.
With no shoes on our feet,
Mondays could be our favorite day.
We could start something completely new that never
existed before.
There would be no strings.
We could look out at the teal sky and forget everything.

All I need is one kiss from you.

We can go at any time.

My escape,

I would love for it to be with you.

TONIGHT

I'll wear that purple dress if you promise to hold me
tight.
I don't need flowers or a heart shaped necklace.
All I need is you.
No matter how cliché,
I promise you that's all I'll ever need.
I'll meet you where the tide comes in.
Under the moonlight is where I'll wait for you.
At midnight we'll go swimming though the sign
says "No!"
If we get caught, we'll run hand in hand away.
I don't care as long as I am with you.
I've waited so long to feel the way I do.
My heart skips a beat every time you go to kiss me.
When I hear a song that sounds amazing,

I don't want to listen without you.

I never truly knew what love was, but I have a feeling that this is it.

Our story is better than any fairytale.

I'm thinking the two of us are going to last.

I'll keep my hair down though I have a habit of tying it back.

Insecurities no longer plague me,
and it's largely because of you.

Tonight, I just might say those three words I was scared to say for so long.

Tonight, I hope you tell me that you feel the same way.

ONE DAY
COMPLETELY MY WAY

One day completely my way:
I'd make sure it was deep within the fall.
In love and deliriously free,
that's how I would want it to be.
Every tear would be washed away.
The sky would of course be dark blue,
no matter the time.
Everyone would find something to be passionate
about,
no matter where they are.
All day you would be able to take in the scent of the
morning dew.
Peacefully consuming,
the strongest salt air would flow through,
like streams of sweetness.

I'd wear an emerald green gown.
A dream it would be.
Orange and red butterflies,
seagulls soaring above, singing their song,
all that is genuine would be present in this day,
this day lived completely my way.

ALL THAT I AM

I am:
Steel drums in the islands,
dancing with a soft breeze.
A Broadway Show at night,
walking out into the city lights.
A country concert under the stars,
right up by the stage.
I am a girl snuggled up by the fireside with her Jack
Russell Terrier,
a notebook and pen in hand waiting on lines from the
soul.
I am a two in the morning windows rolled down cross-
country road trip,
getting out of New York.
And I am:

A red dress girl,
going on a date with you,
an entire being filled with romance
and a hopeful heart that you will truly see
All That I Am.

LIGHT IT UP

I'm so tired of the stale,
let's light it all up
in a shopping center parking lot.
I want to see life in your eyes!
Yes, you who are hunched over,
unable to look up
with bags of groceries in your hands
and exhaustion written all over your face.
I understand.
This is how I came to the color of dark blue.
When the lights go down the magic seems to come
more easily to you.
It's a time for restoring.
I want to bring this to the day,
to those light blue skies too.

I long for us all to see
every minute,
every day,
we are living our story.
It shouldn't be routine.
It shouldn't be ordinary.
We are extraordinary!
We're capable of creating such goodness.
I'm tired of the stale.
Let's light it up!
No matter where you are,
it's all there within you.
I ask you, please,
open your eyes and heart
today!

THERE'S A
STORY THERE

Like a sporadic hailstorm,
Also like the most healing bright sunset,
she's anything but simple;
Full and complete as your favorite flower.
There's a story there,
quite potentially what legends are made of.
Awkward with her words at times,
could describe you or me.

She doesn't always correctly express who she truly is,
but she steadily works toward the person—not version
—of herself that she strives to be.
She's continually climbing to each new ascension.
She doesn't want to miss a single spectacular
experience,
often going to places alone though she would like the
company.
She recognizes that her life experiences have created her
to be different.
The other people don't need these adventures like she
does.
Like air to breathe,
she at times must be in solitude to keep the flower that
she is in full bloom.
She is always learning more about who she truly is.
She is just beginning to love this forever girl.
Looking skyward with her head tilted back,
she's reveling in the rain pouring down at this summer
night concert.
She knows everything is going to be okay.
She is full of life,
with everything that she is.
There's most definitely a story there.

Purple Bicycle

It's a picture she holds dear.
You gave her the first piece of freedom.
Though you were fiercely protective,
you knew her strength before anyone else did.
Captured in this photograph is a girl much younger,
but the belief you had in her on that day remains in her
heart.
You taught her to believe in herself.

Even though you have gone to another place,
you are still with her,
particularly in times of doubt,
with this picture she holds close of a young girl
standing behind her new purple bicycle.

New York September

I've been dreaming of you.
You're the train to all that is silver and gold.
You glisten in the sunset-lit sky of orange and red,
and dark blue.

Your cool breezes trail my deepest passions.
Soon you'll be taking hold of my spirit once again,
with your soft love telling me it's all going to be okay.
My not completely defined wishes will come true,
different and better than I thought.
Carrying on your winds the energy of rebirth,
you fill our souls with the scent of pumpkin pie and
fresh air,
getting us excited for the holiday season stirring
before us.
Dear New York September,
I love beginning again with you.

Fall

The hues become darker.

The lights become brighter.

Delicious pastry scented candles burn.

Windows are left open as crisp air trails in.

An "Anything can happen" anticipation builds.

Desiring the city,

longing for the country,

you're able to pack your lives with it all now.

MUSIC

To the ivory keys
of blues and jazz,
the heart lights with you.

To hear is a gift,
granting a lift
in all the spirit longs to do.

VALENTINE'S NIGHT

The wind roars outside,
melting snow on the ground;
excitement builds waiting on him to arrive.

She wears a short long-sleeved red dress under a black
winter coat,
and strappy black heels.
Soul plays on the stereo.
She brushes her long hair once more,
and touches up her pink lipstick.

The music is turned off with a click.
Silence.
The heart beats faster.
And then-

The doorbell rings.
You on the front steps.
A bouquet of roses in your hand.

Your smile and the look in your eyes when you see her
is positively everything.

To Be Someone

She wants to burn so brightly.
Life—
That's what she wants to be.
She never wants to be someone who people say she was
for a while.
She wants to be fire on a cold night,
the Atlantic Ocean encouraging others to run in on a
hot summer day,
or when life simply gets too restricted.
She wants to be a reminder that you are you,
and that no one can tie up your soul.
She wants to be loud,
and soft when the hearts need this too.
She wants to be...

She's going to be—
Bright!
She's splashing her favorite colors up at the newly
risen sky.

The Artist's Heart

We're all just little girls and boys,
overtired dreamers
high-speed driving the free time as far as we can go,
scribbling in our notebooks between the
moneymaking monotony,
calling up the fairy dust when we notice it slightly
slipping from our view.
We lay the magic in different places,
a promise to ourselves to go and find,
to keep our souls alive,
to make the change only we can believe in.

A Footprint
Was Made Today

Open highway,
a late afternoon sun shining the long way home,
but she's different coming back now,
somehow sparkling a little more now.
The road must have risen up today,
because she's on another side.
She never could have predicted

Feeling these emotions trickling from her head down
to her toes.

It's one of those marks on a life story.

Her character just got a new look.

She found one of the missing notes on a song she had
been working on.

The melody sounds so much clearer now,

so much prettier now!

Yellow roses welcome her back home,

lifting her into another level of beauty,

re-affirming what her heart is already telling her—

"It's time to step into the bright!"

Because she's ready now,

from a footprint that was made today.

MY COLORS

Please give me the bright—
Light!
Yellow Sunflowers,
Red Roses,
Love—
Let it all fall into me,
spreading in every direction,
like a firework,
but electrically silent.
Let this emotion fill my entire being with the most
intensely warm glow.
I don't want the meek.
I need to see this story for myself.
Could it be that I've been told wrong?
Can romance really last?

I'm choosing to believe so.
The neatly designed doesn't appeal to me anymore.
I don't think this way of thinking ever did illuminate
this true wildflower.
I have been scared for so long.
I've been deleting and editing,
unaware of the yellow and red petals turning white.
That's not my color.
It's not my life that I've too often
masqueraded.
I see now.
I'm getting a little louder now.
I'm becoming a little brighter now.
There's a vision of soul stirring yellow and red
always having been there,
inside,
waiting for me to pick up the brush.

BLIND LOVE

I can't place it, but I can't shake it—
This feeling of wanting you when I don't know
enough about you.
Then again,
maybe I do.
Just like me,
you're too free to be defined so easily.
Your messages lighting up my phone sets my mind
spinning so wonderfully.
You have my heart going from steady to a quick beat.
I don't know how you do it, boy.
You make me feel alive, and you're not even here.
You've got me needing you
and wanting you.
And you must know that it's not the attention.

I've been flattered before.

There's something real here.

Any other guy who challenged me so boldly would have been quickly gone,

but I must confess that I kind of like the way you push me beyond fears I never thought I had.

I don't know how to place it, but I can't shake it.

I'm so open to you and this blind love.

Her Exit

She's tired of living under the ruler of consequence.
Her heart is moving,
like a two in the morning New York City goodbye,
because she can't handle any traffic jams.
She already sees herself in his arms,
just the thought makes her dizzy with happiness.
To be fully free,
to get lost,
with him she knows all these possibilities could be.
All the mandates and standards served their time.
Her pretty little spirit is aching so deeply.
She's beyond ready.
Wanting to go fast without any fear of a crash,
him meeting her sooner than she thought,
to go together forever into the sunrise.

She will wear that short white dress,

his soon to be favorite.

They will go so far without any judgement calls.

She has waited so long.

She's ready to make that turn.

She's ready to go!

Your Kiss

Beside the pit of amber flames,
under a black summer sky,
the stars were missing because they were scattered
everywhere in my heart that night.
I tasted the ice cream from the date before,
and my face was blushed in the glow.
You kissed me.
And it was then that I was lifted from one place to
another,
never to go back again.

Always Comes Back

Rocking between two states of being,
lists were made,
and drive was written all over her face.
Then,
your song came on.
You sang of two bodies colliding,
and her schedule flew away
into
The Sound
to the extraordinarily basic,
to simply wanting and needing you,
so soulfully.

Everything I Want

Chocolate-Dipped Strawberries
Iced Sweet Tea
Colored Leaves
An Autumn Breeze
Christmas Sweaters
Fireside
City Shows
Red Dress
New Adventures in Foreign Places
Red Flowers
Open Land
A Great Big Sky
Pink Gloss on My Lips
Full Days in The Ocean
You Hold Me

Water Laps into us as We Kiss

Wet

Love

So Soft on Barely Covered Skin

Festivals

Laughter

Running Hand in Hand through Carnival Streets

Summer Night Anthems

Lighters in The Air

Salt on The Winds

Art Everywhere We Look

Art in Every Breath We Take

A Life We Make Our Own

Everything with You

It's Everything I Want

PART 2: IN THE DISTANCE

YOU DON'T KNOW

You don't know death,
so deletion isn't given a second thought.
You don't know rejection,
when everything and everyone has given in to you.
You don't know love,
for you leave when someone doesn't match you
exactly.

You don't know faith,
to think only of yourself.
And you don't know me now,
when you reach out for a hand that all along would
have been there.

I Didn't Know

He was a take-you-by-surprise kind of guy
with deep blue eyes that erased all reasons to ask why.
I didn't know this now hollowed-out heart I'd come to
feel.

The music that came on did not feel coincidental.
The emotions I shared, I believed were not on rental.
I didn't know this now hollowed-out heart I'd come to
feel.

When we kissed it was obvious that the connection was
deep.
And I had no fear of taking any kind of leap.
I didn't know this now hollowed-out heart I'd come to
feel.

Oh, I can still see his smile and feel his touch.
And it's so hard to move on with memories as such.
I didn't know this now hollowed-out heart I'd come to feel.

A Castle Wall

She's building a castle wall around her heart.
If she could dig a moat, she would—a border not to
block out, but to protect her heart from the
temporary.
This girl is so tired of being a costume,
someone to be worn and experienced for a while.
She never manages to meet their mark—she doesn't fit.
When she gives all her care to each and every one
of you,
she doesn't understand the utter dismissal.
She couldn't do the same to you.
"People come in and people go out," she has been told
time and time again.
"That's just life."
If this is true then, she wonders,

how can anyone truly matter to anyone else?
How can anything be real if throwing it away can be
done so easily?
She used to see every person who came in and out as a
gift.
Now,
she just feels the hurt,
the foolishness for trusting,
the ripping,
the tearing.
And so now she says, "No more."
She doesn't want the temporary any longer.
That is why she is building this castle wall, if only in
her mind,
to remind her heart,
"Enough is enough."

Upon Success

He's baffled by those who haven't even come close,
tearing down those who have worked to achieve the
most.

When you reach for your star, it's almost guaranteed
that Belle's storybook village will never be far.

With jealousy and bias often being what reigns,
whenever it's success that another has gained.

It's such a shame.

It's Too Late

Don't flare up when you read her heart,
the lines are from your carelessly thrown dart.
You disposed and deleted,
in your illusion of enlightenment,
denying the truth of entitlement.
You proclaimed faith,
gratitude was your attitude,
trending along the self-help latitude.
So on and on she writes these pages,
because when it's too late to reconcile,
the hurt must be driven away in stages.

More than
an Opinion

Confidence is good when stirred by the heart,
it is lethal when driven by entitlement,
and thrown as a dart.

DROPPED

I'm no good at letting go. It's a skill I really wish I could know.

I wonder if the hurt ever goes away, or if the twinges are here to stay.

There are times I awake in the middle of the night, your leaving me without a single reason why, still takes the largest bite.

Knowing that you most likely don't think of me at all, I long for the days before the fall.

And if I could only go back, I would have never told

you my heart's secrets that were laid out before you in a
stack.

WRITING YOU AWAY

I used to write your name so differently,
with softness and care,
not with a script filled with sharp edges and fast loops.
I used to take adoration and pride in where my
thoughts went when I thought about you.
But now, this heart bleeds out all over the page,
splattering this way and that,
until there's nothing left to say.

FLASHBACK

I picked up the phone,
I cancelled our plans.
Ten years have passed,
but I'm still picturing the light on the summer road,
waterside dreaming,
the trip that could have changed everything.

Flashback,
turn back,
to the excitement I felt initially.

I could have taken a run.
I could have taken heart rather than fear.

But I picked up the phone,

told you I had to cancel our plans.

Ten years have passed,

but I'm still picturing the light on the summer road,

waterside dreaming,

the trip I really believe could have changed everything.

Don't Tell Me Now

"Don't tell me now," she chimes.
Not when I've begun dancing to a new style.
Not when I've resolved us to the past.
Like thorns on a rose growing into each other,
those last days were scarier than the first ones of
change.

I clearly knew then,
at the end,
what I was allowing to happen to my heart.
Still, I waited too long to play my part,
to say goodbye to you for my first real start.

"Don't recite now the poetry of what you thought we
could be."

Your sentiments and intentions have no weight,
this permanent scar keeps me from accepting the bait.
You are not and never will be
my fate.

FALSE START

I didn't know much,
but love I felt
in your softened touch.

It took storms and such,
for me to see clearly
the need for the clutch.

IF ONLY

I heard you called and wished I had been home.

I still remember the sweet gesture you made.

Given another chance, I'd not let this love fade.

Do You Miss
Me at All?

I often do wonder if you miss me at all,
or if the strong feelings you claimed simply subsided
once your decision had been made.

I wonder if you miss my smile,
the way I miss your beautifully sincere, seeing-into-my-
soul eyes.

Do you still imagine the kiss that never was, knowing
how amazing it would have been?

I'd like to know if you remember the way I blushed
when you first saw me again,
like I recall so vividly the way you didn't look away,
saying without words that you wanted to know every
piece of me.

I wonder if you think of my shy attempt at blowing
you a kiss,
the way I can't forget your sweetly assured one to me
first.

Do you remember all our talks, and not wanting to say
goodbye?

Where did that all go?

I can't stop myself from asking "Why?"

I still wonder in the lost moments of the day and night,
do you miss me at all, or do you think you did me a
favor by letting me go?

I must tell you that the answer is "No."

DEEP LOVE

Didn't quite make it,
did we?
Crazy to think of when you looked at me
like your heart was a book I had rebound
intricately with golden thread
more passionately each stitch.
It's true.
You knew how much I loved you.
Why in the world would you let that go?
Sentiments galore,
each one I hung like a precious ornament
to show all the visitors the many ways you made my
soul smile,
now they are just objects packed away with the deep
love I thought we shared.

Corporate

I'm leaving now, such expectations—they deceitfully promise to own your very soul.

For I have seen their work, in the calm they lurk, stealing your ideas takes quite the toll.

Tearing apart love, in loss of vision, you tend to forget, this is not my role.

FIVE YEARS GONE

I miss what could have been.
Shifting back and forth all night,
you came into my heart again tonight,
making it want for the words you will never say.
I couldn't get comfortable no matter how I tried.

I reread the letter in my mind all the time.

I honestly swear I thought this would bring us back in
truth,
showing how much I really did care about you.
We began by writing our hearts,
covering the distance.
I thought this would help us through the more
difficult times of today just the same.

I never meant to hurt you,
but now here I stand in the middle of this field
knowing you'll never come even halfway.

I miss what I thought we were.

I've spent so many hours writing lines,
trying out different arrangements to get you off my
mind.

We had different passions, but I thought our hearts
were beating together and would be aching when
broken apart.

White daisies and red roses, I never thought we would
be five years gone, never to return.

WHY I WRITE

You've never before seen these words I write,
to you they have come with the harshest light,
shining deeply into the hurt with all their might.
For it is not the words that are so rare,
but the heart popped onto the page that creates such a
scare.
Feelings have been transformed in a maze-like way to

decode emotions that could never be placed on
ordinary terms.
Until now it has been temperance that I have
pridefully declared,
but that left no place for the sadness that the memories
bared.

TO THE LAST GOODBYE

I could fill a book with all the times I have tried to
write you off my mind.
The bad decision of having let you in, still calls to me
every day,
making my heart work overtime to turn the sting into
artful passion that will not stray.
Because you see,
I can't transform the wrong to right.
I can't make the darkness bright.
And I cannot change how the soul saw and then felt
this sight.
When you have been betrayed, letting go is the most
difficult of all.
There are no answers that will be granted that could
hold any reason or rhyme,

and so somehow letting go happens for the sake of
your precious time.

Why?

Why did I play that song?
It was a favorite of mine.
I swayed back and forth,
singing along,
flirting with you.
I tried to bring you into my world,
where the right sound lights a million nights,
but you were firmly planted in your own land.
You only allowed a corner for me,
I can now see.
Now, I listen to this song that was mine,
replaced with slideshow pictures of you holding me,
when you did such things.

In the Storm

If I heard your voice tonight,
would my heart hurt less?

If I saw your eyes so bright,
could the wrong turn right?

If I kissed you now,
could we both feel what *was*,
not all that was lost?

STRONG-WILLED

Maybe it's because my heart lives in a dark purple and
deep blue,
in the lighting in a night concert room
where there's a lone soulful voice and the black and
white keys.
There's a yanking in my throat.
The tears are trying their best to come through.
Yet the fight in me knows.
I know my will is strong.
I am right despite the majority living in corporate gray.
This all just hurts sometimes,
to be fighting alone in a world you see but not many
others can.

YOUR ONLY CHOICE

"Success is the best revenge."
That's what the people say.
The truth is it's the only justice you'll get
since the people who hurt you feel no debt,
nor do they have the soul to regret.

THE PROBLEM

Maybe stop treating people like they're disposable,
replaceable.
Maybe then there will be less violence in the world.
Did you ever think of that?

A DREAM

Sometimes now it seems like a dream,
the relationship between you and me.
It's the kind where all I do is fall,
while you just stand around.
When I wake, this is a memory I can't shake.
So I spend time
looking to find
whether this is simply a dream,
or if you really could be that mean.

WHAT BECOMES

If the love is true,
there is no need for chasing.
If the love is simply attraction,
it won't be long before you'll be
acting.

Johnny

I remember your voice so clearly,
and the way you would abruptly move when
something excited you.
It surprises me that I still have so much to say
about you.
I guess it's because there was a dance,
and many nights with you by my side.
We were two fiery stars amongst a dozen,
both shining differently than the rest.
That's why I still don't understand why we had to say
goodbye.
You knew what made me insecure.
I knew what made you fearful of the time passing by.
Do you know how rare it is to feel the same beat?

So many years have passed with an entire book written about you.

My heart has healed, but the wound is still very much there.

You must know that the hole is wide open,

but where there was pain,

an empty chasm now remains.

SKIPPED STEPS

She gave you the key to who she was from the start, it wasn't for you to let yourself in the doors she had locked.

Strategically moving through her,
you put up the front that you weren't judging her for
the experiences she hadn't had.

She laid out her deepest fears to you,
and intimated quite a bit too.

She thought if nothing greater, you would still be
friends.

You were going to be her city-lights-slow-dance,
holding her close,

A Monday night concert in town,

Her hike along the trails east of Reno to catch a
glimpse of the wild horses,

Or simply the man sitting beside her to watch the
game she never before cared about. That would have
been perfect to her.

She wanted to give all her love to you.

It's such a shame you needed to skip so many steps,

that you didn't care enough to wait just a little bit longer.

WHAT SHE WANTS

It's not complicated at all.
What she wants,
she wishes to have come naturally,
for your ground to have broken when you met her.
You were bestowed an earthquake of a feeling
that cannot be explained.
This feeling cannot be rationalized,
but you should know this is it.
No matter how much dirt inevitably comes in,
the unexpected tearing apart of the vision you initially
saw;
you know there's no one else you would rather tread
through it all with.
What she wants is a love so strong and destined,

a love that never wavers from the 'why'
you took her hand in yours.

Falling Out

I told her
it's the silence
that destroyed
all that we were,
this push and pull
of red desires and white.

CRAVING COMFORT

She lusts for—
the sound of bare feet on tiled floor,
whispered wind,
soft summers,
steady rainfall,
a slowly burning fire,
and embraces that hold beyond the pressures of time.

After—

Slamming doors,
work boots,
vengeful voices,
the three in the morning turning key,

and the bitter taste of being witness to years of a
missing love.

Observation

Last night she dreamed
of a man
who could never biologically belong to her.
With charcoal skin,
he brushed and braided her blond hair
as if she were his own.
With precise but effortless care,
there wasn't a sliver of a doubt—
This was a father's love,
not like her own.

Of the Same Mold

It was not that she couldn't stand to be corrected.
It was the way you twisted your mouth,
and that glint in your tiny eyes
she had been exposed to many times before.
She turned her back to you
and without a word walked out that door.
You finished off your performance with a smirk of
satisfaction.
You thought you had zapped the star you instinctively
knew she had been reaching for.
But there is no defeat in the heart that is no longer
facing you,
please be assured.
You can't afflict her anymore,
now that she has been gifted understanding.

How were you to care when you're made of the same
mold that has never broken?
There are generations of you
oblivious
to the callousness that stirs your many unfortunate
followers.
The dreamless people,
she feels sorry for you.

GETTING OVER YOU

She thought of a remedy,
to list the incompatibilities,
the many valid reasons the two of you could never last.
But when she picked up her pen,
it felt like a weapon,
not a tool.
And it was never her intention to hurt you.
For all the differences in the world
could never erase
the love that left a definable trace.

I'll Take My Broken Heart

I hope you're feeling lonely tonight
and at first you can't even figure out why.
Let these emotions of yours rush in,
with breaks in between,
steadily entering your very cold soul.
I want you to feel the hurt in your intact and still heart.
I want you to frantically search.
Maybe you'll try to put a band-aid on,
but I hope you break down still.
I want you to be shot with the reality that we don't
have forever,
as you carelessly feed yourself.
But I don't want you coming back to me when the
work is done.
You didn't value me,

and I knew from my past that I had seen this before.
Right now, your kiss is slowly fading from my
memory.
I'm letting the memories fade,
and I'm genuinely grateful for my broken heart.
I know,
the pieces will be put back together,
completely differently,
with a touch that truly cares next time.
But for you...
I really do hope you're feeling lonely tonight.
I hope you break down when you realize how much I
cared for you.
And I hope you remember every kiss and every touch.
This is not for me.
I want this for you.
I hope you remember,
and that you appreciate the next girl who comes
your way.
One in a million,
that was me,
and she will be too.
Once hurt,
I'll never return to you again,
but you need to realize,
none of us have forever to make it all right.

THE LASTING ONE

She heard about the coming storm
and she drew open her dark blue curtains to see.
The way the rain changes over to snow,
the way a heart goes from racing to a steady beat,
there's such a transient nature to it all.

And she begins to think that maybe she just
desperately wants a certain touch,
arms that want to hold.
No matter how strong the memory,
it all fades just the same.
And it scares her that nothing lasts forever.
That's what the people say.
But she believes that there must be something that
transcends,
when love is real.
That has to be the one piece of magic that stays.
'Till we meet again,'
there must be such a thing.
For the power in the pouring rain,
there's such energy to the sky at times like these
And she thinks of somehow and somewhere,
there just has to be a lasting one.

A KIND OF LOVE

Someone is always waiting,
left hurting and missing.
That's just the way it goes.
It's the magic that turned,
something he or she must have never seen or known.
It's the theme of you and me.
And I can't forget,
like you forgot me.

Everything you were in my heart,
I write the words down,
but it's the same message every time,
and it's all about you.
You'll always be in my heart,
a story that will always be unfinished to me.
And I guess that's how some stories are left to be,
that one someone waiting on that chapter,
when suddenly they are reassured that it has always
been two.
But the phone doesn't ring,
and that's just the way it goes—
one day, maybe.

DIFFERENT SIDES

I wish it wasn't this way,
between you and me,
pulling on opposite sides of a long, thick rope.

My spirit seems to be rooted from yours,
but there are days when drawing away from you is all I
want to do.

I don't know what to believe,
how to feel about you.

Sometimes you seem to care,
but other days there's such darkness inside you.

Some things seem unforgivable,

but still, *forgive*, we're told to do.

Fearful of naivety,
I don't want to excuse and abuse my heart all my days.

"Right" and "Wrong" is never clear.
It's always gray around you.

And there isn't a moment,
a day,
or time, when I don't wish—
I really wish it wasn't this way.

SAME OLD STORY

It just takes a few strings strummed on that electric
guitar.
Her heart racing,
beneath her bedroom spotlight.
It just takes a few high notes coming from her stereo
tonight,
and she'll be gone!
So, fill up your assigned seats.
Tweet it...
Facebook it...
Blog it...
Enjoy it!
It won't be long.
When the storm clouds come,
she'll be moving on.

When you realize that every day will forever be
achingly the same.
The path you glorified,
it's now your prison.
It's the same road you were on when you looked to the
left and shook your head.
You made her feel misplaced,
and she almost swayed.

GIRLFRIENDS

She didn't know the power she had,
for the girl—to her—was nothing but a temporary
space to fill,
that steady girl who at a crisis would come running
every time.
All the songs written,
they're all about romantic love gone wrong.
But what about all the other kinds of love?
Nothing more,
but nothing less.
Two best friends:
A kind of love that can sometimes hurt the most.
When broken,
it can be the worst of all.

When secrets were shared,
and stories that were meant for just two,
now just a runaway with chapters of you.

Unplanned
Attraction

She promised she wouldn't fall for him.
That was something she didn't need.
And yet...
She can't seem to get him off her mind.

Sweet kisses play all over again.
Arms wrapped around her,
holding her tight.

He played by the rules they both set out.
There's no reason to be waiting by the phone.

She told him the kiss wouldn't change a thing.
Living in the moment,
it all seemed exciting at the time.

She told him she didn't want anyone tying her down.
She agreed with the sentiments he shared
before this whole thing even started.

A wild heart,
never truer,
but she knows that she still desperately wants to feel
close,
to know someone cares about her too,
for someone to need to hold her at times,
someone out there who she thought could have
been him.

She promised she wouldn't fall.
That was something she said she didn't need.
But...
She can't get him off her mind.

PIECES

Fragmented memories
piercing,
whether it's day or night.
And I can't understand why we can't be whole.
These flashes prevent sleep.
I'm replaying everything unmistakably right.
The wrong...
there's nothing there,
nothing that matters anyway.
We had a love so believable to the heart.
We had it all
it seemed.
It kills me that your touch cuts right through me still,
a little bit more each day.
But you don't come back to me.

And you must see it too,

the two of us were beyond this earthly existence

in a Heaven of our own imagining.

If we could just push through these brick walls,

I'd take a hammer to everything blocking our way,

breaking all the insignificant issues piece by piece.

I'd let it all go.

I'd throw it all away

to be in your arms again.

My world would be complete.

A meant-to-be we have.

I know one thing for sure,

we're not supposed to be in pieces.

IF ONLY YOU KNEW

I can hear the sax coming from the apartment
downstairs.
It's playing me the blues tonight,
"If it's over, let me go."

If only you knew,
I never planned on falling for you.
Seeing you every day,
I saw you as a friend,
and nothing more.

I didn't know you had liked me since day one,
when we first met in that class we had together,
for it was only a few months ago you told me.

Suddenly, details I never saw,
they became as vivid as a blue flame against a black sky.
Your ocean eyes I could no longer resist.
Your charm made me smile even through the darkest
days,
and when you'd look into my brown eyes,
you made me feel beautiful for what felt like the first
time.

If only you knew,
it wasn't your kiss that sealed my heart.
It was the way you rested your hand on my hip
and pulled me close.
It was the way you reached for my necklace,
looking at each charm as your fingers touched and
lingered.

I felt safe with you.
I trusted you.

What a mistake!

You had to know right from the beginning,
I wasn't like the girls you normally dated,
how every moment meant so much to me.

Honestly!
What were you expecting?

I just love how you think I can go back
to being friends with you—
slapping me on the back
like I'm just—
"One of the guys."

Forgetting every word,
every touch,
every kiss.

The sax continues to play as I sink deeper into my
covers,
rainy stars sparkling through the window.
And my mind keeps feeding me wishes
that cannot and will not come true

If only you knew.

FALSE LEAD

I almost got caught!
All the notes matched up.
There was the thrill of uncovering something new,
testing me just right.
All signs pointed to you,
but you were just a false lead.
You got my heart beating for no reason at all,
and I was all too ready to take this fruitless chance.
These past emotions of mine now making me feel like
a fool,

but I know so many others have traveled down this
road too.

I'm sorry that this is a comfort to me today,

this all too ordinary road we've all traveled down.

It could have been a battlefield,

but I made it out just in time.

Your tantalizing moves danced the line,

giving this smart girl just enough doubt

as I watched from that safe distance,

the flames rising all around what I believed was meant
to be.

Irreconcilable

Snap!
Our relationship is finally a wrap.
You laugh,
it has been over for you since the last call.
I'm aware that you don't think of me at all.
It's okay.
It took me longer
to piece the truths together.
Early morning hours,
awake in the winter-dark room,
I twirled around the hurt in my mind.
I thought about the audacity,
that you could live the way you do,
with all your lies,
when suddenly I heard myself from within yell,

"Stop!"
The lightbulb clicked on.
It was my turn to laugh now,
at myself.
How blind I have been to ignore the glaring reality.
Irreconcilable differences,
if we were legally bound,
that's what would have been declared to set us both
free.
There are justifications you have made that I could
never wrap my head around.
I am not perfect,
by any means,
but there has been so much self-inflating,
while you profess your honesty.
It took me all this time to see,
how different you are from me.
And now,
I'm so happy that I can finally say goodbye.
Snap!
Just like that,
our relationship is a blessed wrap.
For I know who I am,
And I know who I am not.

I WOULD HAVE STAYED

I feel like a screenwriter.

All too often I draft lines in my mind.

If you said this instead of that.

If you hit your mark here not there.

But human beings are not puppets on strings,

they're more complicated than that.

Even so,

one thing will always be true.

If you had let me into the pain and confusion you were feeling,

I would have stayed.

I would have assured you that everything was going to be okay.

I wanted to stay.

But you,
you pushed me away.

A VISION OF MORE

You really missed out.
You told me that my face was one you could get used to
waking up to.
And with this confirmed vision from you, I drew in on
this future image,
like a film that puts you right in the scene.
I had it all laid out.
I could see everything...
The first house,

Walks in the country up hills and through the
wildflowers where I used to go many years ago,
Live concerts, holding your hand.
I even saw the mundane as great with you.
I would do the dishes and the laundry you so disliked,
and you would do the cooking I hadn't found my style
for just yet.
We would work together.
You even told me you believed we could.
I saw no fantasy without the realities.
Loves who hadn't worked out before,
I knew I could be the one to open that different door,
to a love you had never experienced before.
You really missed out.
I had a vision of so much more than what we got.

Intimacy

You tried to take her under
like the puzzle-master that you are.
Not once did you pause for the corner pieces
to tell the story that shapes the full picture.
These essential pieces,

they're the key ones she needs to hear you say "I love
you" to.
You think she doesn't understand.
To you she's just thinking too much.
But what you experience in minutes,
she's been emotionally exploring for years.
She has been uncovering unmistakable results,
if she lets go of what her heart is saying.
No matter which way she turns,
she unravels one solid truth.
There will only be regret if she says "yes" to you,
no matter how she wishes she could,
no matter how lonely the time is
down in her soul.

PAST, PRESENT, FUTURE

She misses you,
all the more these days.
And she wonders,
how did this happen?
All she can think of is that she never signed the waiver,
yet time kept moving on.
When the heart remains in the old picture,
it's unbearable to let go.
When the feelings match the "Then" better than the
"Now,"
what can you make of the "Today" and "Tomorrow?"
The past,
present,
and future vision,

it's all mixed up
while she decides on her next move.
But the camera always captures the "Here," "Right
Now."
So, wise men say, "Let's make it count!"

MAKING IT A LONG ONE TODAY

The hurt and excitement are jumbled together today.
Tying up my shoes under the hot sun,
I'm setting out with a determination I haven't felt in so
long.
I'm going to take in the scent of pavement and land.
I want to run through the confusion,
Into a deep light.
A lot of uphill is what it's going to take.
I'm going to keep going as I become more of myself
with each stride.
I'll run until I can no longer feel any sort of ground.
I'm making it a long one today.
A melody in motion,
I'll keep going until there's nothing left but heart.

I won't worry about getting back by a certain time.
I'm letting the clarity come through.
This one is for me.
Today,
a long one is what I need.

WAITING IS THE
HARDEST OF ALL

I wish I could take your pain away.

I know, because I have felt the same.

Everything is snowballing out of control, you say.

You're *tired of being the disappointment*, you claim.

You don't fit in with those who surround.

You incorrectly think there's something wrong
with you.

You have such an urge to scream out,

"This isn't fair!"

The person beside you is trying to keep you calm.

"Don't overreact."

"Things will change."

"Things will get better."

But "things,"

things remain the same.

You sigh.

Stuck in a rut,

sometimes waiting is all that you can really do.

More often than not,

you have to keep reminding yourself that you're

stronger than you feel right now.

You're stronger than you feel right now!

One day soon, please believe me, you will see that your

strength is true.

You will see soon that you have made it through.

I'm telling you that I felt the same as you but made it

past these wild emotions.

You are stronger!

You are remarkably stronger than you feel right now.

PART 3: UNHINDERED

Ego

There is a title that irks me like no other.
You'll never guess because it's proclaimed by a plentiful
number
and their brother.
"Self-Made" is the term.
Please don't squirm.
I may have caught you!

It's okay to be one of them too.
So please let me explain by stopping the rhyme here.
I want you to understand why I feel how I do, dear.
Here is the truth,
I believe no one gets anywhere completely alone,
for someone had to say "yes" to you at least once
before.
It is the ego that wants to take credit for everything.
But it doesn't matter what you do, someone else had to
have at least a shred of belief in you.
We are part of something so much bigger,
whether you have faith or not.
We need to take care of each other, you see,
for a life is made up of a you and a me.
There are the roots, branches, and leaves,
but they wouldn't exist without the seeds.
So please don't say that you are self-made,
since it's only through caring for one another that we
are truly paid.

#MeToo

I can guarantee we've all been there.
Her stories may be subtler than yours,
but a young girl doesn't forget something like that.
It's when she wised up just a bit more.

The day her boss picked up his cloth napkin and told
her she could wear this in the pool, said it in front of
his wife and a few other women who just grinned and
shook their heads.

Or the time this other man told her she had a very
"down home" look and shouldn't be afraid to wear her
hair down and a top that is of a lower cut for a job
interview.

These experiences taught her to never stay with
remarks like that.

She's stronger now in wisdom and beauty too,
protecting her value even more.

She believes that there are many more men who aren't
this way,
but it's also thanks to the examples set by the brave
women who sang "Me Too."

Our sincerest gratitude goes to you.

TIMELESS TRUTH

Sharing,
in magnitude,
mountain-peak majesty,
seems to exist
only among those atop the first hill.

THE FIGHTER

He's a mix of training
and heartbreak.
He comes at his opponent
with eyes as cold as ice.
Only through a deep connection

can you see the truth.

There's a desperate need to win,

not driven by ego,

but by one too many times being told that he's

nothing.

Watch him work.

He's going to show that he's really something!

Unbeatable.

Unshakable.

With a vault of experience,

he's a fighter

building the intensely real love he once felt back up

again.

ECSTATIC

Yellow leaves are splattered on fated branches.
There's a quiet noise within—
A knowing,
the you-of-before
is the you-no-more.
Landscapes have changed.
Hurt made the heart beat—
wildly.
Blooming into the winter,
you're everything you dreamed you'd be.

CHOSEN TIME

Love me in the morning,

most of all,

before your eyes have adjusted to the day,

when the sun comes too quick,

too bright,

and steps and answers are met with a cold silence;

for it is at this hour and state of being,

I will know for certain,

what we have is true.

With Me Always

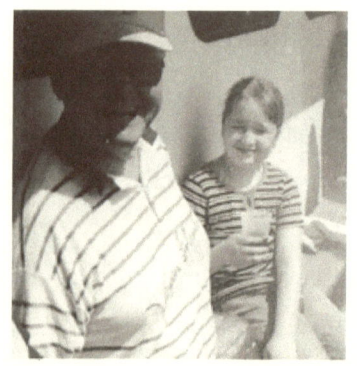

Your height is still clear.
Your face a blank slate,
yet your encouragement I feel,
a strength from you.
I miss you.
And in my heart, there's a calling,

to take the next step in my life,
maybe because the colors of you are anything but dull.
Instilling the deepest jade in me,
I see you watching over me.
Your strength lives in me,
with passionate shades of blue too,
inspiring shades of red,
and empowering shades of purple.
Your hand is on my shoulder.
I feel you guiding me,
more now than ever before.
You are with me always.

HOUSE OF MEMORIES

At home with the old walls,
the lightbulb that is the first to go out.
Put me in any room-
the place that has seen life,
the most heartbreaking,
the most dangerously intoxicating love,
I want to sit with you.
I want to listen to your story.
Please tell it all to me.
There was a time,
not too long ago,
I wanted to erase it all and make everything new,
completely sterilize all the darkness created by you.
It may sound foolish when this is impossible to do.
I wanted to make it easier to forget all of you.

Now I see,

I wouldn't want to erase any of the moments.

I don't want the perfect anymore.

Everything right wouldn't have led me to the way I feel right now.

I feel unmistakably right,

right now.

The broken pieces being put back together in a whole new way.

I finally see beauty,

a kind I have never seen before.

I didn't think this happiness was possible.

Tonight, I want to thank you.

Tonight,

I want to look back as well as forward,

because there's a peace I have gained.

Now I realize I couldn't have made it here without you.

I'm going to be alright.

I'm going to be better.

Dusting off the boxes,

don't turn on the air or open the windows,

I want to spend my night with you,

where the paint is worn,

inside this house of memories.

Just Being

Suddenly, I am completely aware...
The movement of my foot—
The way my fingers shift as I write—
The white curtains in this hotel room,
and the way they ever-so-slightly dance—
The sound of the water running...
I can See!

And Hear!
And Smell!
And Taste!
And I can't help but be amazed.
And I wonder why we let ourselves become so
overwhelmed—
Impenetrably sad at times.
It's remarkable to feel this hunger.
Even in my emptiness,
there is still hunger.

THE CHALLENGE

Pushing up that hill,
let the others walk,
slow and steady,
saving their energy for the final stretch,
when the others notice.
That's not worth the win to me.
What gives worth is something greater.
It's in giving it everything you have—
When the rain is pouring down,
the mud is splashing up,
the muscles and breathing become weak,
when you feel as if you can't make another stride,
but you keep running.
You go strong all the way,

leaving nothing but your heavy beating heart in
the end.

Win or Lose are superficial terms that carry no
meaning then.

You completed the challenge.

It's something not many can say.

It's a strength many will never gain.

It's a real gold medal
that can never be taken away.

NEVER GOES AWAY

In the storage room of her childhood home,
she holds her soft pink satin pajamas—
Princess Jasmine.
Still carrying the scent of summer vacations long ago—
air conditioning and chlorine,
a favorite piece this had been.
And she realizes now that this had covered a heart—
Her heart,
that thankfully still beats the same today.

HER WILD HEART

She's taking this beautifully chaotic life one turn at a time,
one straight away
come what may.
A soulful electric guitar down one path,
the patiently steady piano keys the next—
Collaborating together.
Playing the music of this wild heart,

it's a never-heard-before melody,
and never will the notes be the same again.
This messy and sharp sound,
that is also soft and feminine,
this song is filled with early heartbreak as deep as the
ocean,
and love as passionate and enlivening as the touch of
the first autumn breeze on sunburnt skin.

UNSCATHED

Please hand me your story—
pages full,
not just the black and white,
but the browns and grays too.
Place it on this table,
and let it all go.
I have something to share with you.

There are heartbreaks of mine that I would color the
same as you.
For every tale that you have,
there's someone out there whose story is different,
but with parts that hurt just like I'm sure yours do.
I only say this for you to understand that you are never
alone in your pain.
I only wish for you to know this truth.
This life is full of stars and bright colors,
but no one lives without the other shades too.

Where To Go

On this same road again,
but making different turns.
None of us are given the map,
yet somehow we're all led back
to the one place
with the one road
where we each individually have our own.
It's where the most painful times have been.
It's where innocence and truth remain.
If you don't know where to go,
you must go back—
to pick up the unresolved
in acceptance and understanding,
in strength and gratitude,
in happiness,

and in love—
to spread flowers,
so that no matter where you find yourself,
when you're truly on your way
your heart will always know where to go,
and where to stay.

THE WAY I AM

There are a dozen pictures,
numerous sides to show,
but you often choose the ones I think aren't pretty.
When we first met,
I tried so hard to be the kind of girl I thought you
would be attracted to,
but the winter wind blew my hair into tangles,
and the grime of the train made my face flushed and
worn,
yet that was the girl you fell for.
You saw me the way I am.
You saw this as beautiful.
I told myself many times that I would learn to wear
more makeup,

to take on the appearance of a woman who had it all
together,
to be what I had learned from magazines and other
women in my life,
but no matter what I do I still see me,
and I'm beginning, just beginning to see this as
wonderful.
Because you have always seen me,
and you have loved me deep.
And this version of me you say makes you happy.
I would do anything to make you smile.
You see me like no one else ever has.
At my most vulnerable,
you love me just the way I am.

HER SUNRISE

Orange,
yellow,
pink
brush strokes in the blue-lit clouds.
All with no set technique,
only following a feeling.
Little did she know this feeling was received through
the sound of her quiet longings.
The poetry in her heart was heard by you.
So that early morning when she decided to seek her
answers on the road like she used to,
you had your beautiful show all ready to go.
You brought her right back into the girl she truly is.
Like the heart-beating-body slipping back into form
after a coma,

she was given another chance,
a new life with the girl who has always been there.
This girl never required society's validation.
You set the clock back,
to the girl who can't stop being enamored with the sky
above,
and is at home on the open road.
This is a girl who needs to be in love.
For the past few days, her mind has been running wild,
consumed in intoxicatingly
sweet imaginings of him holding her like he said he
would love to.
She put his words on replay to remind herself that
someone truly wanted her.
But at the end of the day,
she's alone.
And at times this has made her feel lonely and worried
about the time passing her by.
So, she had to venture out again.
A traveler,
looking for experiences,
never stopping,
she needs the deep and lasting in everything
with her right here and right now.
It seems you, her sunset, were sent just for her.

Wrapping her in your intensely powerful shades,
"I'm constantly changing, and I will never leave you,"
your colors seem to say,
with an echo of, "You're not wrong to believe in what
you do, and to desire it all too."

SHE IS FREE

She is rarely the first out of the gate running,
though she would like to be.
Her spirit is strong,
but her story is different,
and always has been.
She's in this journey for the distance.

Hundred mile-markers give her such a thrill,
and her heart builds up with more emotion than any
other of her kind.
She takes in every detail,
the in-between colors of every sunrise and sunset,
particularly the ones the others don't notice-
the shades that haven't been named yet.
She falls more.
She must work harder.
And she is often steered into loneliness
to learn and listen to this state's breath,
to feel this emotion through her entire being and sit for
the truth,
the real love in this pain.
She will often appear as if she will never fit into this
place,
and then suddenly...
out of the sweet rains she garners such strength from...
you'll see her running at record breaking speed!
She becomes even more of an enigma than before,
but she is free,
and happier than she ever thought she could be.

LETTING GO

Lost photos,
the missing notebook,
the ones you thought were here to stay—
Letting the unresolved wash away.
It's never simple.
It is a day-to-day drama until you don't want to carry
the ache any longer,
those memories that were never meant to be forever.
It's then that you let it all disappear into a fun beat,
making your soul want for the completely different
entirely.
You get back on your feet.
Those past entries,
photographs and certain people,

you suddenly understand that they can't apply to the
journey you are on now.

You are on a path that can only have the genuine.

You let the truth encompass your heart now.

From here on into forever,

finally,

you see that you're completely ready and able to let go.

LOVELY

The opening of a single red rose,
the mist of a Tiare flower in the late autumn air,
a long satin dress softly hugging her body,
the touch of your smooth lips on her neck,
your large hand entwined with hers,
a whisper of the truest love,
a few strands fallen loose from her hair all done up
for you—
like a painting
with drops of rain on black mascara,
a sparkling sea blue heart necklace,
simply knowing forever is with you—
It's all so lovely.

A NEW YORKER

A New Yorker I will forever be.
No matter where I roam,
the rhythm and soul of this place steps with me.
A darker horse it makes,
wild and free.
It sees everything and is difficult to twice deceive.
It has taken me a long time to see,
the armor I now wear doesn't come for free.
I know how to work hard for everything I achieve,
and show you exactly what I can do and what I am
passionate about.
The strength I have garnered here leaves me with just a
little less fear.
And as my grandfather would always say,
"Work makes the living sweet."

My One

If I were to paint you a color,
you would be yellow—
warming my heart,
lighting my soul,
giving hope when at times I feel I don't fulfill any role.
"That couldn't be further from the truth," you would
stop the world to say to me.
My hands in yours, you'd look into my eyes to ensure
that the words from your lips I wholeheartedly see.
And you would never tire from telling me so,
as I too would try to pull down the stars and moon to
make sure you know.
For you are my forever,
and it is this steadfast belief in you that I know will
never sever.

KISSED...

By love
on that date to the ice cream place.

By faith
at the crowded concert where a stranger held my hands
as "I'll be there" played.

By inspiration

when I realized I had made it through the most life-
altering storm.

I may never have been in love,
but I have been kissed.

Many times,
I have been moved beyond compare.

RECAPTURED

I remember him
like snow in the heat of summer
taking me there,
a spirit that never goes away.

I hold him close
with a picture on the bay

many years ago,
his smile in my heart remains like the most brightly
shining ray.

Poet

I feel so alive when I put the pen to page.
A strike of inspiration comes down in pearls,
one at a time.
It's just a few words and I feel touched by grace.
Kissed with a power much different than any that have
touched my lips,
I am set free.
I'm given the ability to create magic from what existed
between you and me,
no matter how tragic it may have all seemed.

HER LOVE

Beside a white piano in a sparkly dress,
that's where you'll find her
singing out songs that spread from one being to the
next like glitter.

In a tiny jazz club deep in the city,
she's in the only home she'll ever desire,
beside a white piano in a sparkly dress.

Singing out songs that spread from one being to the
next like glitter,
swaying in the intoxicatingly sweet present,
that's where you'll find her.

WITH A GRATEFUL SOUL

With a grateful soul
I write
of all the changes that have made me whole.

New Year

She's a surfer,
race car driver,
a mover,
dreamer,
and believer.
Always turning the temperature up,
she's hot to the touch!
Sweet the story would be if you were to come along,
but her chocolate-stained grin can't wait.
Awakened one early a.m. by a twinge
under a tropical night sky,
her heart was shocked by the cumulative time her smile
was tucked so far away.
Brown eyes softened their sultry sparkle

till she saw the scribblings of how this year almost gone
has changed her.
Beneath the dance of palms and painting of stars,
she opened a new room in her soul while much of her
world was still resting.
Decorating this space genuinely,
she let in very few this time,
accounting for only an additional two.

LIKE NEVER BEFORE

I want to fiercely love,
with the kind of love that can only come from above.
I desire to hold you tight,
and yet never hinder your flight.
This is all because you bring that secret smile to my
face,
making my time feel sweetly endless rather than a race.
You take me without hesitation on every water park
ride.
You have me continually longing for midnight swims
by your side.
My heart wants to fiercely love you at outdoor
concerts,
within fireside talks,
on road trips to no-place-in-particular,

anywhere and everywhere,

for what we have is rare.

Like never before,

there is no keeping score.

You brighten my days and never fail to give me all that

is more.

A Part of Me

I think about all of you from time to time—
Every single person who has entered my life,
whether for a number of seasons,
or just passing by.
I often recall the connections made in a stranger's eyes.
You are all a part of me,
like one of those crocheted blankets my grandma
made—
A gorgeous array of colors sewn together from thin
pieces of yarn,
keeping me warm.
I don't need to think of you every day,
the simple beauty of you remains.
In happiness or hurt,

your significance is known.

You influence my story,

whether I can place you or not.

And this is why I will always proudly say that I am far
from self-made.

INSECURITY

It's probably one of the key emotions I feel.
When your path is opposite the rest,
your patience and belief are really put to the test.

But I am here to tell you that the stormy days do clear,
making you wonder how you could have so
profoundly doubted yourself, my dear.
All your passion will eventually be completely seen and
gratefully received.

So don't let your insecurity get the best of you.
This is an emotion that never fully goes away,
but it also tends to be the backdrop of the stories that
shine the brightest ray.

THIS SWEET LIFE

Spring is birth, most times a little uneasy,
but just like the cherry blossoms bloom,
the sweetest sight wouldn't be as great without this
awakening light.

Summer takes hold of your emotions,
giving way to delicious getaways and long days on the
water,

warm nights under the still sunlit sky, and then the
gorgeous view of moonlight, stars, and fireflies.

Fall will always be where the work of your story takes
hold.
With the scent of pencils, the sight of colored leaves,
and feel of crisp air,
the heart is uncovered under dark blue skies and in knit
rainbow-shaded scarves.

Winter wraps you in family and romance,
having you embrace the most important of all
in a rose red, silver, and white, by the yellow glow of
the fireside.

THIS GIRL

She identifies with the two-in-the-morning leave
Pink tulips
Red roses
Sweet Tea
Kissing on the rocks
Strong hands on her hips
making her want to sway back and forth
with you
Bright sun shining down
Ocean waves storming
Sunrise or moonlight
Private city night
Electrified light
This girl is only scared of losing the fire
She's a biting-her-lip flirt,

Eyes sparkling,

Over-the-top happy,

Deeply sensitive.

Fast car

top down

Craving that immortal feeling

Cruising down a lane of golden reeds

Saxophone

Drum Beat

Electric Guitar

The Voice that reaches into your soul—

sounding beyond the back wall

This girl wants for nothing but a great and intensely

true love—

one that raises this earthly place a bit above where it

has been

BURNED NEW

This summer,
she's burning off this old skin.
Her hands are going to have a whole different feel.
She has been hurt and made it through.
She's fearless now.
This soul of hers has been tapping like a steady
drumbeat,
now the music is coming through loud and clear.
Wild and forever young,
she knows what you've all been looking for,
but she made her own list,
and she's ready to run for each mark.
Suntan lotion shimmering on her skin under the
hot sun,

she's pushing through any tired feelings.
For the birth of this woman she has been waiting on,
she's breaking through.
She's setting herself up!

THE REGRET I'LL NEVER HAVE

It's the one regret I'll never have.
I don't withhold any feelings I have ever had.
But more love than hurt you will always know.
I put myself on the line every time,
no matter how broken I become inside.
It's something I willingly do,
not just for you, but me too.

It's because my soul cannot bear to give my heart only
partially.
When I love, I have no brake,
I love all the way,
no matter what, for me,
is at stake.

PRETTY STRONG

The years have taught me a lot.
What stung with such bitterness at the time has helped
me navigate within the place I am now.
There were nights I longed for what felt impossible—
because it was
at the time.
There were days I wanted to shut out the sunshine,
and I did sometimes.
Every experience consistently told me to put the pen to
page,
feel these emotions completely,
let it pound away until I am able to break through,
transforming these life gifts into a gorgeous reflection
of the human spirit.
That is what I hope to do.

There was no shown door.

"Precisely," these voices of mine would agree.

"You're building the door."

It all seemed so exhausting, but I defiantly listened.

I was never promised the path would be easy.

I'm glad it wasn't

I was never told whether I would see the fruits in a
month or a year.

I now grin at the ten years it took.

What these inner voices in me did though, was pull me
toward the sweetest and most enlivening songs amid
it all.

In music, nature, and the smallest of children,

I found my encouragement and continued inspiration.

And I became stronger, living in this ache of the heart.

It turns out I made it through strong enough,

understanding fully the need to continually climb.

It's true that the most wonderful takes time.

WITH YOU

Within me there is so much to give.
The most powerful capacity to love has been pent up
for years.
There was never one who had me the way I see you do.
Magic carpet rides and wishing on stars does not
remain fantasy with you.
I can feel the heights,
and there is no emotion of fright.
You are grounded while taking a great liking to the
clouds above.
A dreamer just like me,
I have every desire to take care of you in the deepest
way,
making sure our love always burns bright.

Because only with you I see my happiness becoming complete.

For you are my last remaining puzzle piece.

ALIDA

She wears:
gold,
red,
sapphire,
gowns that hug her body.

She laughs:
at convention,
subsidiary roles,
and the prevalently unevolved.

She leads:
with her heart,
soul,
and knowledge of human nature.

She lives:
with nobility,
grace,
fearlessness,
romantic freedom,
ambition,
and openness.

She speaks:
kindness,
questions,
constant hope.

She seeks:
relentlessly,
to go beyond,
and to forever vanquish any drops of darkness.

She is:
passionate.

HER SPIRIT
ON THE PAGE

Tapping out the rhythm on computer keys,
it's obvious there's wildness where she grows.
Dream catchers made of wood and fallen feathers hang
from small trees.
In the distance a soul-driven drum beat hits in perfect
time.
Wind whistles over mountainous canyons.
Frayed golden brown hair flies.
And she runs
from one view to the next.
She's consumed by love and excitement for the land
before her.
This is where she fits.
And there's a man.
She can see him,

as if he were holding a torch to light her way.
He embodies a spirit much like her own.
Inhabiting both boy and man,
he is never one without the other.
He sees her,
the girl and woman beyond his dreams.
Brown eyes lock for the first time.
And it's only the beginning.

THE ARROW

I've got that sexy soul,
a country love song,
and city dance pop,
playing the soundtrack of my heart.
I'm thinking about that body-hugging sparkly dress,
the one that makes it tough for my guy at the end of
the night to say goodbye.
I'm not one to love in parts,
one day deeply-felt letters,
the next, not even a text.
This is why I'm now finally seeing which team I'm
leading,
and which one I need to stop continually feeding.

YOUR INNER STRENGTH

There's something about returning each day to what
cut at your heart,
not in acceptance,
but in passion for what you believe.
When you feel that you can barely control the tears
that want to fall,
you take a deep breath.
When the desire to quit is strong,
but the devastation of this action would be greater.
When deep down you know,
God is letting these circumstances happen for an
enlightening and heart-filling reason,
yet to be revealed
when you power through.

Fire Sign

She lets this electric guitar and passionate voice direct
her every move.
She wants to get absorbed in the pain it took.
For he sings of the emotions that currently have her on
the hook.
Endlessly longing for this high that is so thrilling,
she's melting away any restrictions under this blazing
spring sun.
The light is ahead and behind.
She's consumed by the wild,
working the missing out.
Desiring a dive into the expansive deep blue nearby,
iced water fills her lungs back up.
Her convictions are stronger with each stride.

To be completely alive,
she runs for this.

To Go Back

To go back,
not in the encompassing time,
but to tiny moments,
to place a firm and grateful hand on what still haunts.

Twilight tears
dripping in the hollows of my heart,
I yearn to once more stand in that hotel parking lot in
Colorado
before the first-seen mountains
breathing the fresh air my lungs had never felt before,
taking in the early morning sun
before my family came out with the rest of our bags.

Maybe I'd like to see that boy's eyes again,

filled with attraction,
and feel his fingers slip ever so slightly from the
dangling charms on my necklace
to my skin.
Maybe it's wrong to want such a thing,
for this didn't end so well when truths were shown,
but I can't help but hold onto that feeling of being a
rose.

I would also like to walk down the street from my
aunt's house again,
absorbing the freedom,
like dozens of lightning bugs rushing around inside my
soul.
It was the first time I was allowed to walk alone
to the white horse that lived at the last house on the
street.

I would like to touch these memories again,
to fully inhabit the magic that my life has already held,
and fill up the well of power within me
to know with unwavering courage,
there's much more to come!

IMPERFECT

There's a perfect version of yourself
you'd like the world to see
at all times.
Never too skinny.
Never too big.
You cover up all flaws.
Don't look too innocent.
Watch for the snakes.
Watch for the change.
Never let anything slip you up.
Because you feel the swords from others,
yet none go in as deeply as the one you use on yourself.
But when you stray from the absolutely genuine,
the moment always arrives
where you're scared to make any move at all.

You disappear.

You give away the chance of becoming the legend you dream of,

the legend you saw.

So that is why today I sign to the imperfect,

the up and down,

the "ugly" with the "nailed it" shots.

To always be sparkle.

To always be love.

To always be delightfully imperfect.

HER ANSWER

Silence she took,

when witness or subject to injustice.

Then it was letters and articles when she could take no
more,

received with utter dismissal or anger.

So now it is forever poetry that is her chosen course,

her final resolution.

Moving diagonal to the snakes and dragons,

she understands that they will always do their thing.

But "I" who am "She,"

a poetess at heart,

shall eternally string lines together under jasmine filled
nights.

With a band of like-minded souls,

I will try my hardest to overpower the darkness,
pushing love to the front of your news,
and be a promise of light that you can always find.

YOUR PEOPLE

There all along.
Repeated gems.
You see now.
The ones you thought you wanted,
never were true to your soul.
Showing their lack luster color through empty seats,
their absence made the atmosphere more alive.
You realized to your surprise,
there were no gaps in your heart tonight.
These true ones glimmering with unmistakable love,
you recognize your people now,
no longer looking out in the crowd for what you
thought.

TEEN SPIRIT

Too young
Too old
Too different
to feel this love
to understand
to transform
Everyone is saying
"No."
But below the night sky
the field lamps illuminate a summertime
Running around circles of the past
when convictions weren't easily replaced
with confusion
There was a hope that tomorrow could bring
reinvention

even if today hadn't gone so well

Painting your white walls bright red

there was an identity even in the unsteady

This is a time and age that passes

But this is also a spirit

A spirit remains

A spirit that stays within

This is a magic that can become a part of you again and again

at any time and at any age

"Yes!"

Orange Sherbet

You have me thinking of orange sherbet
like gloss on the lips
bright in color
sweet going down
cooling the center of my forehead
where too many drifters live
clearing my being
like the summertime
and new love.

MARCH

There's something about March
and the last icy night.
The wind is quiet,
an after-the-snowstorm kind of silence.
The cold air is taking center stage,
but this time you don't hurry inside.
You breathe the chill in,

allowing winter's goodbye to exhilarate your heart.
Overwhelmed in the best way,
you're tingling from your head down to your toes.
And you feel immense gratitude,
for this intensity,
the life in these changing seasons.
As the crisp air dances on your skin,
through the black wool coat that will soon slide to the
back of your closet,
you come to the most satisfied conclusion—
It is true,
you are fully and completely in love with life itself.

SAGITTARIAN SOUL

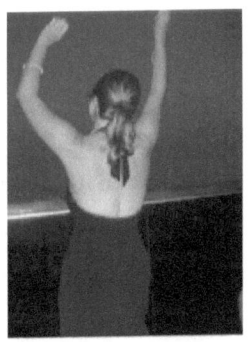

She's tired of chairs and mattresses,
structure of all kinds.
She wants to sink into the sand and feel the grains
between her toes.
She wants to lounge high up on the jagged rocks,
overlooking only ocean,
and out to the heavenly sky.

Neither here nor there,

yet deeply engaged in the pursuit and commitment to a wild love,

a love that keeps her reaching,

for all the many ways she's destined to be.

She wants a love that is unhindered,

passionate,

beyond this world.

This is a love that lives, breathes, and seeks the grandest heights.

It's a love where you can jump off the cliffs just to prove what remains,

what is true.

And it is everything.

The heart bursting with more love than one can hold alone,

That is what she forever desires in her Sagittarian Soul.

PART 4: DARK BLUE ENCORE

Just Like That

Neon pink and blue
reflected on the night water
from the city towers.
Little did she know
her new life was about to unfold
as the sun would begin its ascension
on the port of call across the way.

PRETTY

I wish I had as much insight into me, as I do you.
A cameo confidence,
I come in the fitted gown at times I could never
predict.
There's no question of makeup,

I see myself truly without any embellishments that fail
to speak to the heart.
But there are many more days without this strong
identity.
I see you,
much taller than I,
and a body that would look great wearing anything.
You have full hair, and the red lips I often wish I could
pull off without looking like a fool, an imposter.
So why do I hear you say that you desire to look just
like me?
This tale seems to be recited all the time.
Why can't we all see our own "pretty" permanently?
Instead, we're just pretending until we genuinely
believe and
finally see.
Pretty You.
Pretty Me.

MISTAKEN IDENTITY

I didn't know my own truth
when I fell for you.
Black leather and mahogany cologne,
you were strength and security
when I hadn't found my own.
Breathing in lavender,
in a yellow sundress,
I'm holding in my soul
everything I now know.

THE ELUSIVE MARK

A feeling so deep that it immediately emboldens the
heart,
like the last lap, with a competitor trailing an inch
behind,
you win,

because you have that *something extra* driving you past
where you and others have gone before.

This is what inspires.

Like that part of the song that's so sharp and
unexpectedly reached,

you are lifted high each time you hear those notes
conducted.

Nothing less than passion,

this indescribable feeling that you long to bottle up
and channel on lesser days.

It's the sign that you are here to push past the pain and
doubt for a distinct reason—

For your true potential and the fire in your soul.

Achieving greatness that extends beyond yourself to
reach others,

it's legendary status.

And it's why everyone begins to sing your song,

follow your art,

your uplifting actions,

and go to your games—

Tears fill their eyes,

arms reaching out as far as they can to the stage you've
been given.

It's the elusive mark anyone can find,

but few do.

It's where our purpose lies.

My One Sweet Memory

I want to remember you just like this.
My boy,
you were my best friend.
Standing in my living room,
I'm holding the memory right there.
We were locked in an embrace.
The outside world gone—
I thought it would last forever.
Your goodbye
wasn't real.
You even carried the sweet flavor that took you
from me.
We held onto each other,
and I knew it wasn't just me that felt this—
to know that you have loved someone so fully,

so completely.

I remember you like this.

And I know you cared for me too.

Left to the ethereal we are,

and our connection is strongest in this farewell memory

repeated in my dreams from time to time.

I wonder if you share this same dream too,

remembering me just like this

—like never before—

neither of us stronger than the other.

It seemed this embrace was a culmination of all our days.

You will always be my New York home,

something I no longer want to deny.

We are the broken good.

Somehow this is just our story.

Still With Me

Coming back,
looking back,
I never thought the memory would go this far back.
I still feel like that girl
wearing the gray skirt with the thin pink band around
her waist,
blue sweater,
long boots,
and hair tied back in a low ponytail
walking from class to class in this different place,
a world away from New York, yet I felt safe.
The romantic life was alive here on the pure and
beautiful land this campus was
built upon.
I never blended,

I didn't care.

There was freedom in that.

Country love songs were my soundtrack.

Ten years have passed,

but I feel the same when I go to bed at night.

Kansas was a core part of my being that came to life for such a brief time.

This unique place is within me still,

like a compass now

providing direction for where I should go next.

JOURNEY OF FAITH

This narrow dirt path of autumn-covered trees
at times takes her down
to a place of desperate dreams.

The way the desires marry themselves with the rhythm
of the wind,

she can't put her heart aside.

She is blind and pleads for the right ground.

Running one stride at a time,

a sudden opening of seagrass stalks begins to change
her perception.

She sees grace as the wind coasts slowly through her
being.

Love is what she suddenly feels.

She notices a collection of faces in her mind's eye—

Family,

Friends,

People just in passing—

How blessed she is!

She suddenly sees.

She has been given all the threads,

finding within and leading her to all her desired
dreams.

When looking up in this moment at the spectacularly
sea-colored sunset,

she notices

the path before her has widened.

WARRIORS FOR LOVE

We're the warriors for love,
as the others look on with doubt-
The "realists,"
suppressing the innate
with the notion of honor.
But they fade away just like all of us,
only differently,

with no pangs in their hearts.
Never broken,
never to be filled with the greatness that streams in
after.
While we warriors for love wear the brightest shades,
and a shocking honesty.
We take chances.
Because you only get one true love.
But you also get a dozen and more moments,
many memories.
And we tend to see more in that which did not fit.
We love the same,
through the tears,
even when we're screaming out against the lessons,
longing for something right to come through.
We know,
this love is most definitely worth the wait.
We know settling brings much greater consequence,
The damage doesn't as easily subside.
This we know for sure,
that we must fight when the heart is in its greatest pain.
There's a love we warriors will always believe in.
And for that belief
—and faith—
we will attain much more.

More than what could be imagined,
more than any dream or fantasy,
we are given so much more.

She Holds On

She holds on,
to the flowers you gave her.
Petals pressed in a journal by her bed,
easily torn, she touches them lightly.

She holds on,
to the other side of the coin,
where the bitter is traded for the few pieces of
wonderful,
for the true love you gave her that shouldn't be tainted
or taken away from the heart's memory.

She holds on,
to the knowledge that only one is meant to go the
distance.

She holds on,
to what remains,
to the good in you that will forever light her soul in
times of doubt.

And she holds on,
to this genuine love she has for you.
Always and forever,
this will remain.

New Beginning

The weather has drastically changed.
First day of the clocks having gone forward,
and the snow is quickly melting outside.
Could it be that I am both excited and terrified?
It's well past five in the afternoon,
and light blue shines through my curtains.
All in the overnight it feels like,
I am solidly ready

to stop resting,
to live almost erratically.
That is the level today.
I feel like taking a bite into the sweetest clementine,
and running the roads I had previously fallen on,
not worrying about a thing.
I used to love winter the most,
but my life is changing.

THE "NOT MY TYPE"

You shimmered across my mind tonight
like dozens of tiny stars in a black sky.
Your presence in my life was so profound,
though you probably never knew.
I never told you.
I don't think I even understood at the time
how lucky I was,
for you weren't "my type."
But a song brought you back to my heart,
and I realize you never left.
You were one of the first to know the soundtrack of
my soul,
and you let me know in action and interest that I
wasn't the only one.
You brought to life the melody behind the words,

feeling these emotions just the same as I did—
I know.
I don't believe anyone else ever did.
You have married another,
but what a special gift you have given me.
Never to be taken away or tainted,
your love is of the lasting kind.
The memory of you makes me continually feel special,
and worthy of a great love.
And I want you to know,
though the stars for us may not have connected just so,
you were and are a great love of mine.
And I wish from the deepest part of my heart that you
always stay true to you,
and know that the "Not My Type" that you were fits
perfectly in my heart and memory to this day.

You'll Always Have Me

What will be, will be,
because you'll always have me.
Sometimes you must take what you need to breathe,
and let the fires burn, not seethe.
It's an uphill heartache, I know,
but it's better than living in a mistake.
To be free you have to let go,
and take with you only that which you know.
But no matter what the fates have in store,
I promise you'll never be left waiting behind my door.
What will be, will be,
but you can forever be certain you'll always have me.

Starting Now

I'm going back,
starting over today.
I'm erasing practicality,
it's no longer any use to me.

I'm going to put that cotton candy flavored lip
smacker on,
lie down at the top of the old track bleachers,
and simply stare up at the sky for hours.

I'm going to dream of the rain,
and a kiss in the middle of a Kansas wheat-field.

I'm going to have it all right now.

I own a heart that no one can stop from beating.

I'll go back.
I'll go forward.
I'll go wherever I want and create my place.
I know it's up to me.
I'm starting now.

Breaking down today,
I'm going to build something new out of the old.

Today I'm going back,
I'm going to think about the things that used to mean
the most to me.

Falling in love,
living the adventure,
making a difference through words—
through music,
my dreams are going to come true.

No one will be able to hold me down.
It all starts right now.

Dancing

She heard your song in the distance,
the one that can only belong to you,
and she began to slowly stroll by the shore
with the casual sway of her hips
and a twirl placed just right.

A young girl who's now a woman,
she's the silhouette in the beach-soaked sunset
remembering your touch
and the way you matched so perfectly with the electric
guitar solo.

You made her feel alive.
And like a tattoo, you rightfully remain on her heart.

She reflected on how deeply you wanted her in
every way.

She let this reality dance with her all these months
later, into the night.

Tears have dried to a smile of grace and pure happiness,
and she sees you now as the gift you were—
feeling blessed for the time you loved her to this song—
a song that is everything she was to you as well.

To the Beat
of Her Heart

She's driving away tonight from the race,
to where she can feel her own unique pace.

There are too many distractions
when she reveals herself only as a fraction.

With red roses and the music of a saxophone taking
her high,
she can't settle with just a slice of the pie.

And because a thicker skin doesn't get as far as you
would think,
she's relaxing into her emotions and avoiding this
circular rink.

Rolling on into the dark blue,
to the beat of her heart,
from here on out she's trailing only the true.

SOMETHING IS COMING

Driving along,
staring out at the light denim-blue sky,
I believe my life is changing.
A freedom song,
a siren on my radio,
there's something about to unfold.
I believe,
soon everything will be revealed to me.
Sweet kisses are crossing my mind,
and a melody that melts deeply inside me.
I'm leaving any bit of doubt on the outside.
I hear violins slowly sliding through a soft drumbeat.
I hum along,
trailing through an inner maze,
and cruising the lines.

I'm longing for a big heart to come and take me away.
I want someone who is passionate,
someone who feels an impulse and does not hesitate.
I want a compatible heart that not only needs but
wants.
I don't want anything temporary.
I don't want the easily-fading.
The rain begins to fall,
and I believe,
something is coming...

In Color

Messages come through
like the sound of rain.
Gentle signs
direct me in which way to turn.
There's a devotion in seeing,
nothing is up front.
Looking within,
there's a lot to be discovered.

Taking the time,

with sparks of the soul,

I receive an explosion of pastels.

Sharing a message of love,

I know that's what we were sent to do.

Always something new,

we continually need to follow through,

in color.

WHO'S WITH ME?

The circumference around you silently vanishes when
a song that speaks to you
comes on.
You avoid the news since it's always filled with the
wrong kind of blues.
Everyone who touches your soul has the potential to
become an entire story.
It takes you a long time to move on from a kiss of any
kind.
It's even harder to get a dance off your mind.
You dream of wildflowers and fresh Wyoming air,
not to mention those New York City rooftop nights
with a loved one at your side.
You're endlessly grateful for the tears of yesterday

knowing that this has definitively shaped the person
you are today.
You are too sensitive,
sometimes rash,
but everything you do comes from the heart that you
wear like a sash.
Everyone can see.
You're at times misunderstood because you bottle up
those feelings for far too long,
but like the freedom-loving half-man, half-horse of a
certain sign,
you keep moving on.

BROTHER

How did you do it?
You always convinced me there was nothing to it,
everything took just reading and doing.

You have continually encouraged me to try the new,
and you have always looked at me as if I already
possessed the golden ring,
never doubting my ability to sing.

In your eyes I have been the superwoman I desired
to be.
You don't see me as a little sister, so teammates we
became in an
at-times battle that kept changing its name.

I wouldn't have it any other way.

You brought poetry to me first,
before any other guy stepped in,
introducing me to jazz and country on those long
cross-country drives.

It has always been just the two of us,
roommates and best friends.

And whenever you sensed my fear of the next
adventure becoming too great, you knew the exact
rhythm to play.

We have never been in competition with each other,
but I have always wanted to be like you.

You are my big brother,
and you can be certain that this love I have for you is
the one thing that will never change.

My Painted Trillium

You are my Painted Trillium,
a wildflower that's shaped almost like a dart,
you don't do anything without a passionate heart.

You're a woman who hasn't left the girl behind.
A tie-dyed-pink center splattering out into the white,
shows the without-barriers-creativity of your mind.

Never strong without a great amount of the delicate
too,
you stand out because you are brightly true.
Rare if not impossible to find anyone who comes close
to you, you are everything I want to be,
Mom.

ALISTAIR

There's a Jack Russell I'd say I know pretty well.
He has me well-trained without the use of any whistle
or bell.
Anyone who has this breed understands how I fell.

He's a clever one, my little guy,
with quite a bit of style in his file.
Donning bow ties and sweaters,
he's an about town kind of fella.
My angel on earth,
there's not a single doubt that heaven sent him down
to be with me.
I adore all the funny games he plays.
He loves me unconditionally,
curling up so close to me,
to my heart he forever has the key.

FINDING FLORENCE

She was love through security and routine,
making sure I had everything I could ever need.
But in pictures and glimmer-in-their-eyes stories, I find
the much larger side of her,
the side I saw the moment we lost her.
She had that same mischievous and enamored-by-love
grin I am said to have.
I can't forget that smile, and it's what I choose to be
important to remember.
A terrible disease took her,
but even in forgetting,
her determined strength shined through.
It's one of the many character traits I hope I continue
to gain from her.

She was one of the first women to work for the United
States Trust Company on Wall Street.

I would like to think that my configurations of words
come from games she adored too,

since it's definitely not the skill of math I have
inherited from her.

In these black and white photos tonight, I am seeing so
much more.

I am discovering a glamourous woman who knew how
to have fun,

but also took great responsibility and value in how she
presented herself to the world.

I hold myself to this same standard too.

I continue to wear the dresses and sweaters she made,

and I wrap myself in the colorful blankets she carefully
crocheted.

I am discovering more of my grandmother I am said to
have in me, every day.

And I couldn't be more humbly grateful, as I aspire to
this label, for someone who I know quietly believed in
me and continues to do so today.

I truly believe she's watching over me,

in inspiration and love.

OUR REASON

We are the artists,
our existence hung by thin threads of color
in constant movement
to settle where we won't be cut down.
We search for a safe place,
within the globed enclosure of a giant sunset sky,
where we can give our passion to the stars

in wishes to illuminate all the dark places,
forevermore.

ACKNOWLEDGMENTS

I would like to thank my family, here and in Heaven, many of whom are included in individual poems in this collection. Thank you to everyone who has encouraged my writing and expressed how certain poems have touched them personally. I think as artists, no matter the medium, we are looking to put our heart and soul out there for not only ourselves but to connect with each other. It is my hope that my collections comfort, uplift and inspire all who take these books into their hearts and minds. Whispers in the Velvet Blue is particularly special as these poems and their sentiments encompass a time that has long since passed. While published now, these were the poems that came before all the rest. Thank you to my Godfather, Clifford Fischer, who has read all of my poetry and has encouraged me all along, and thank you to everyone at Harbor Lane Books for believing in my work and bringing it to such beautiful fruition. In conclusion, I am so thankful for music that is a continual inspiration, and to God for blessing me with this spark within to share my words and thoughts in this way with you all. Poetry truly fills my heart with so much joy and encourages me to see the spirit in every moment of this life.

ABOUT THE AUTHOR

Christie Leigh Babirad lives on Long Island and is a poetess of numerous collections. She continually aspires to illuminate the moments in life, no matter the size or subject, and create art that will not fade with the passing time.

You can follow her work on social media at the following sites to find out more about her latest projects.

facebook.com/authorchristieleighbabirad
instagram.com/christieleighbabiradauthor
youtube.com/@christieleighbabirad1707
goodreads.com/cbabiradauthor

About the Publisher

Harbor Lane Books, LLC is a US-based independent digital publisher of commercial fiction, non-fiction, and poetry.

Connect with Harbor Lane Books on their website (www.harborlanebooks.com) and social media @harborlanebooks.

facebook.com/harborlanebooks

x.com/harborlanebooks

instagram.com/harborlanebooks

tiktok.com/@harborlanebooks

threads.com/harborlanebooks

pinterest.com/harborlanebooks

ALSO BY CHRISTIE LEIGH BABIRAD

Evergreen
poems

CHRISTIE LEIGH BABIRAD

Lilacs
and
Roses

A POETRY COLLECTION

CHERYL BABIRAD
CHRISTIE LEIGH BABIRAD